God's Ways Are Higher

Treasurers of Wisdom Series
Volume 1

Deborah Esther Nyamekye

ISBN: 978-1-9163509-7-7

DEDICATION

I dedicate the Treasures of Wisdom Series of books to my source of revelation and inspiration, the one and only God Almighty, Creator and Redeemer through Jesus Christ the Messiah. There are no words in any language to express my profound love, gratitude, and total dependence on Him.

He is my everything!

Contents

PREFACE

God's Ways are Higher is a book written for the purpose of taking the reader on a journey into deeper realms in God with inspirational teachings that give scriptural insight into the unique and diverse ways of the God of our Lord Jesus Christ.

"My thoughts are nothing like your thoughts," says the LORD. "And my ways are far beyond anything you could imagine. [9] For just as the heavens are higher than the earth, so my ways are higher than your ways and my thoughts higher than your thoughts." (Isaiah 55:8-9 NLT).

God's ways are not easily understood by the human mind, in fact they may appear foolish when human beings try to interpret them with their limited understanding apart from God. However, God in His Sovereignty as the All-powerful Creator and Controller of the universe always knowns what He is doing. These teachings are inspired by God given revelation from scripture and are either based on case studies of biblical personalities, specific incidents or focus on specific topics with general scriptures that reveal God's ways founded on His principles.

The inspirational teachings serve to give a clear insight and understanding of God's ways or wisdom that affirm ageless principles underlying His actions and manner of governing His people and the world in general. They are also written to teach and encourage or exhort the believer in Christ with the hope of helping them in their quest to be renewed daily with a mind of Christ, therefore drawing closer to God through Christ. The apostle Paul in the scripture below explained that it is only those who arespiritual who can receive and understand truths from God's Spirit. These truths are the ways or thoughts of God. These "spiritual people" as Paul states have the mind of Christ.

"13 When we tell you these things, we do not use words that
come from human wisdom. Instead, we speak words given to
us by the Spirit, using the Spirit's words to explain spiritual
truths. 14 But people who aren't spiritual can't receive these
truths from God's Spirit. It all sounds foolish to them and they
can't understand it, for only those who are spiritual can
understand what the Spirit means. 15 Those who are spiritual
can evaluate all things, but they themselves cannot be
evaluated by others. 16 For, "Who can know the LORD's
thoughts? Who knows enough to teach him? But we
understand these things, for we have the mind of Christ."
(1 Corinth. 2:13-16 NLT).

Chapter 1
God's Ways, Thoughts and Our Obedience

Part 1 Baffled by His Ways? God always has Reasons.

Key Scriptures: 2 Kings 4:8-37, John 14:21-23

In 2 Kings 4, Elisha's servant Gehazi obeyed when Elisha told him to go to the Shunammite woman's home and to lay his staff upon her son who was dead. I noted that Elisha told him to be focused and not to be distracted on his journey, a detail which adds to the reader's confidence that the servant's mission would certainly result in the woman's son rising from the dead. However it did not happen.

One might ask "Why is it that the man of God's staff was unable to produce the intended miracle?" We realise later on in this account that when Elisha and the Shunammite woman arrived at her home after the servant had, Elisha performed the miracle of resurrection by praying, then laying on the woman's son.

Again one might ask *"what was the point in Elisha sending his servant ahead in the first place if God intended the miracle of resurrection to happen in a different way?"*.

At times as Elisha's servant we may know without reasonable doubt that The LORD has told us to do something and He has given us specific instructions on how to do it as Elisha did his servant. However having obeyed God, we do not see any change or godly fruit as expected. The LORD wants to encourage us by reminding us that His ways and thoughts are higher than ours (Isa 55:8-9).

"O the depth of the riches both of the wisdom and knowledge of God! how unsearchable [are] his judgments, and his ways past finding out!" (Romans 11:33 KJV).

There are several reasons why we may not experience or see the fruit or outcome we expect from obeying God, here are two:

1. What we do for the LORD is at times part of a chain of events and there is someone or other individuals who will perform their part in that chain at different times.

In the 2 Kings account, Elisha the prophet's actions were the final stages to the boy's resurrection. We should be encouraged that what the LORD has asked us to do, however fruitless or trivial it may appear to the natural eye or human understanding may be an important part of a process leading to a glorious outcome.

2. What the LORD told us to do may have achieved the outcome to the glory of God, however it was not evident as yet to the natural eye.

God could choose to open our spiritual eyes to it at a later date or not at all. For instance many intercessors have prayed about issues God has placed on their hearts and engaged in prophetic intercessory acts by the leading of the LORD but have not seen or heard evident changes to the glory of God as a direct result of their intercession.

Our part is to be as Elisha's servant, undistracted and focused on our obedience to God and our pursuit of godliness, trusting him all the way. We must rest assured that whatever we do for God through Christ Jesus is never in vain whether we see the outcome one day, never do or the end result is not as we expected it to be. We serve a sovereign God who is in absolute control.

"Who hath directed the Spirit of the LORD, or [being] his counsellor hath taught him?" (Isa. 40:13 KJV).

We who love God are reminded of the rewards of obedience:
"Jesus answered and said unto him, If a man love me, he will keep my words: and my Father will love him, and we will come unto him, and make our abode with him" (John 14:23 KJV).

Abiding in God's presence or glory, as a reward of obedience to Him, should be our priority above all else. It is the key to attaining all that He has for us and being fruitful for His sake every day of our lives.

Part 2 God may choose to go against the Status Quo

"He (Elisha) went in therefore, and shut the door upon them twain, and prayed unto the LORD. And he went up, and lay upon the child, and put his mouth upon his mouth, and his eyes upon his eyes, and his hands upon his hands: and he stretched himself upon the child; and the flesh of the child waxed warm. Then he returned and walked in the house to and fro; and went up, and stretched himself upon him: and the child sneezed seven times, and the child opened his eyes." (2 Kings 4:33-35).

When we think of the unconventional manner in which Elisha was used by God to resurrect the son of the Shunammite woman, (2 Kings 4:33-35) we cannot help but conclude as with other incidents that the Most High God is master of every circumstance and therefore He may choose to act differently in situations which may be the same or similar and produce the same glorious outcome.

With this in mind, we think of how some healings are straight forward in that someone lays hands on the sick and they are instantly healed whereas other healings may take time.

The way the LORD would choose to heal someone may be unusual or unconventional but the result manifests as would a "normal" healing process; a glorious testimony of the healing of God.
Some examples in scripture include when

I. Jesus spat on clay and placed it on the eyes of a blind man, and he regained his sight (John 9:5-6).

II. Naaman had expected Elisha (2 Kings 5:1-12) to heal him in the way he approved of and felt was appropriate. As a man well esteemed in Aram, he was used to being elevated and had a great measure of self-pride.

THE "NATURAL" MAN RESISTS OBEDIENCE

Naaman was offended that Elisha did not come to heal him by waving his hand on the spot where he had leprosy and calling on the name of the LORD, instead Elisha sent a messenger to tell him to go and wash himself seven times in the Jordan. Naaman was also offended by the choice of the river which was Jordan in Israelite territory. He initially refused to wash in the Jordan for he deemed it an inferior river in comparison to the rivers of Damascus until his servant persuaded him to obey the prophet.

Naaman's resistance was due to the fact that he judged by his natural mind; because of the debased value he attached to the river Jordan compared to the rivers of Damascus, he automatically concluded that God could not or should not use it to heal him.

"But the natural man receiveth not the things of the Spirit of God: for they are foolishness unto him: neither can he know [them], because they are spiritually discerned. But he that is spiritual judgeth all things, yet he himself is judged of no man. For who hath known the mind of the LORD, that he may instruct him? But we have the mind of Christ." (1 Corinth. 2:14-16)

This account shows us the dangers of resisting what God wants to do in our lives. Resistance occurs because people do not discern that He is at work as events taking place do not appear normal or they go against the status quo.

"Father, we pray that you would grant us the gift of discerning of spirits, your wisdom and knowledge so that we would know when you are at work and also see things the way that you see them, in Jesus' name, Amen".

FAITH, PATIENCE, AND TRUST IN A GOD WHO IS IN ABSOLUTE CONTROL

When the Shunammite woman and Elisha (2 Kings 4:8-37) arrived at her house after the servant, she discovered that despite the servant obediently laying Elisha's staff on her son, he did not rise from the dead. However, she did not complain, she was a woman of faith and therefore had confidence in

Elisha; after all did not the LORD give her a son through the prophetic word spoken by Elisha (2 Kings 4:8-16)? She also believed that God would revival her son through this same prophet which is why she hastily went to see him when he died.

The woman had faith in the man of God and served him as a result God gave her a son. Likewise, as we have faith in the LORD and serve Him, we are guaranteed to bear lasting fruit (John 15). As the Shunammite woman, we too must exercise our faith and be patient, trusting that the LORD will fulfill that which He has promised however long it takes.

"For as the rain cometh down, and the snow from heaven, and returneth not thither, but watereth the earth, and maketh it bring forth and bud, that it may give seed to the sower, and bread to the eater: So shall my word be that goeth forth out of my mouth: it shall not return unto me void, but it shall accomplish that which I please, and it shall prosper [in the thing] whereto I sent it." (Isa.55:10-11)

We praise God that He is a God of second chances who breathes life into all the "dead" areas of the life of His children.

"Jesus said unto her, I am the resurrection, and the life: he that believeth in me, though he were dead, yet shall he live: And whosoever liveth and believeth in me shall never die. Believest thou this? (John 11:25-26 KJV).

Part 3
Obedience is Partnering with God by faith for His Will to be done on Earth

The prophet or intercessor when revealed the will of God partners with Him to ensure His will in heaven is made manifest on earth. Their prayers and actions in obedience to their call affirm that they are perpetually engaging in acts which are aligned to how the greatest prophet and intercessor Christ Jesus taught His disciples to pray "Thy Kingdom come, thy will be done on earth as it is in heaven". Thus, they are confident of the outcome of events to the glory of God.

As believers in Jesus, we have the Holy Spirit dwelling within us who is also the Spirit of prophecy/Testimony of Jesus (Rev. 19:10). The Holy Spirit knows the mind of God and reveals His will to us and makes intercession for us according to the will of God (Romans 8:26/1 Corinthians 2:9-12) each of us therefore can know the will of God and to intercede for His will to be made manifest on earth. This is our inheritance as children of God.

In the account of Elisha raising the Shunammite woman's son from the dead (2 Kings 4:8-37), we see that he was inclined to use a method which to the natural eyes looked unusual; Elisha performed the miracle of resurrection by the following process (2 Kings 4:33-35):
He prayed to God, then he
-lay on the woman's son,

-took a moment to walk up and down the house for a while, then
-went back into the boy's room and lay on the boy again. This time the boy resurrected from the dead.

Partnering with God in confidence and even in what appears to be peculiar ways for the ultimate fulfillment of His will by Elisha reminds us of Christ. There is a long list of examples in the life of Christ, however we will focus on resurrection miracles of Jesus; He said the Synagogue official, Jarius' daughter was not dead but sleeping (Mark 5:39) and was laughed at by the crowd. When Jesus was told by Lazarus' sisters that he was sick, he said that the sickness would not end in death, but it was for the glory of God, and so that he, Christ would be glorified (John 11:1-4). However Lazarus died. Jesus also referred to Lazarus death as "sleeping" to his disciples.

By the time Jesus arrived, Lazarus had been in the tomb for four days. Mary told Jesus that if he had come earlier their brother would still be alive. Christ knew that there would be the manifestation of a greater miracle and therefore greater glory to God in the resurrection of Lazarus than in his healing, *"so when he heard that Lazarus was sick, he stayed where he was two more days..." (John 11:6).* In both resurrection incidents, Jesus demonstrated himself as the giver of physical life as he is also the giver of spiritual life. (John 11:25KJV).

The attitude Elisha and Jesus had and the actions they undertook in the resurrection process are not easily understandable to the natural human mind. This is because the ways and thoughts of God are higher than those of men (Isa. 55:8-9) "*and because the foolishness of God is wiser than men; and the weakness of God is stronger than men (1 Corinth.1:25 KJV).*"

As Elisha knew it was God's will to resurrect the Shunammite woman's son, so too Jesus knew it was God's will to resurrect Lazarus. Therefore when Jesus said Lazarus was sleeping and took what seemed like a long time to arrive, he was speaking and acting as one who already knew the outcome, which has already been decreed by God in heaven being one with God (John 10:30).

As children of God, we must remember our identity as heirs with Christ which means we are exceedingly abundantly blessed and therefore with a great capacity by the dwelling Holy Spirit to be used for His sake. This includes seeing things the way Jesus did and therefore making ourselves available to be used by God for miraculous works. Jesus even said that those who believe in him will not only do his works but greater works than he did (John 14:12 KJV).

As we live a life abiding in God and He in us through Christ Jesus in the power of the Holy Spirit, nothing should stop us from exercising our faith as Christ did. This includes declaring those things that we know are His will by faith, preaching the Gospel and other works of the ministry (Matthew 28:18-20) and taking authority against Satan and his demons (Luke 10:18-19).

My prayer is that we would know our God intimately through daily bible reading and meditation while in fellowship with the Holy Spirit. This way we will become more like God, speaking of those things that be not as though they were, (Romans 4:17). We will also walk in His wisdom, knowledge and understanding, always strengthened by the power of His might to do exploits for Him. "...but the people that do know their God shall be strong and do [exploits] (Daniel 11:32)."

Chapter 2
God's Ways: Maximising His Glory -Delay is not Denial."

Part 1 Glory maximisation: The Birth of Isaac to Abraham and Sarah.

God did not allow Abraham and Sarah's old age to serve as an obstacle to prevent Him from fulfilling His promise that He would give them a son. If He had, then it would mean that He would be confining Himself within the boundaries that the natural or carnal man lives by. This type of person does not live by faith in God and so the things (ways and acts) of God which are spiritually discerned are foolishness to them (1 Corinthians 2:14).

Perceiving things from a carnal "natural man" mind set results in the conclusion that a woman of ninety years old, which is an age well past menopause, can conceive is impossible. As the angel Gabriel told Mary the mother of Jesus Christ, concerning Elizabeth who was also past childbearing age "with God nothing shall be impossible"(Luke 1:37 KJV).

Our God is the great I Am, the Almighty God also called El Elyon, the Most High God, creator and possessor of the whole universe!! He is a "mountain mover"; no obstacle whatever its size is insurmountable by Him in the pathway of fulfilling

His plans and purposes to the glory of His Name and Kingdom.

Therefore, we serve a God who is as controller of the universe does what He chooses to do and when He chooses to do it. This is why if we choose to be as the Spiritual man of 1 Corinthians 2:15-16, walking in and judging by the Spirit as ones with the minds of Christ, we are guaranteed an understanding of God's ways. True worshippers who worship God in Spirit and truth in these last days are the type of people God calls His children (John 4:24).

DELAY IS NOT DENIAL, BUT TO REAP MAXIMUM GLORY

It is worth noting that it took 25 years before the promise by God to give Abraham a child came to fruition. Abraham was called out of Haran and from among his relatives by God at the age of 75 (Gen 12:1-3) and God promised to make him a father of many nations. He was 100 years old when Isaac was born and Sarah was 90 years old (Gen.17:15-21/Gen 21:1-3).

Through this incident we are given an insight into one of God's ways rooted in His nature or thoughts which is how He strategises a number of times in scripture to prolong the waiting time for the manifestation of His promises or miracles so as to reap the maximum glory out of them.

In the case of Abraham waiting for 25 years before

the son of promise was born, this meant that the extent of awe of having Sarah give birth at an even older age than when Abraham received the promise and the extent of Satan's defeat and the shame rendered to doubters and mockers was far greater than if God had performed the miracle the year the promise was given or earlier than when it was fulfilled.

We serve a multi-tasking God who while reaping the maximum glory out of a situation through a chosen strategy will simultaneously be applying another strategy within the first also for His glory.

For instance, God also strategised that Abraham and Sarah would benefit during the waiting period for their child. They benefitted in that their faith, patience and perseverance in relation to God, His ways and acts were strengthened. God will use every opportunity to transform our hearts and minds so that we become more like Him through Christ Jesus.

By the time Isaac was born, Abraham's faith and trust in God was such that he did not hesitate to commence the sacrificial process of Isaac, his much sought after son when God told him to do so. When he was about to kill Isaac, God provided a ram as a substitute.

God's command to Abraham was a test (Genesis 22:1) and he revealed to Abraham that he had passed the test in this manner: *"And the angel of the LORD called unto him out of heaven, and said,*

Abraham, Abraham: and he said, Here [am] I...Lay not thine hand upon the lad, neither do thou anything unto him: for now I know that thou fearest God, seeing thou hast not withheld thy son, thine only [son] from me." (Gen 22:11-12 KJV).

God also foreknew that Ishmael would be conceived by Abraham with Hagar, Sarah's Egyptian maid due to impatience while they Abraham and Sarah waited on God to fulfil His promise.

Therefore, while to the natural mind Ishmael's birth was an accident, in God's supernatural plan it was not. Ishmael's birth and therefore destiny as a means through whom nations would be born (Abrahamic inheritance, although different to that of Isaac) was God's will otherwise He would not, in His sovereignty have allowed it to happen.

Despite challenges, impatience with God and testing along the way, Abraham prevailed and was imputed with the righteousness of God as well as an all-time recognition as a world-renowned man of faith. Abraham must have been filled with awe and thankfulness (although scripture does not state this) when he contemplated not only what God had done for him and Sarah but how He had done it; God reaped more glory before multitudes out of Abraham and Sarah's prolonged wait for the promise than if God had done it another way and it included increasing this couple's knowledge of the thoughts and strategies of the God they worshipped.

As children of God, we ought to be encouraged by this as we live our Christian lives because at any given time, God has our destinies perfectly mapped out. In addition, as long as we continue to partner with Him, He will fulfil His promises to us no matter how long it takes while removing every obstacle and reaping as much glory out of the process as possible.

Part 2 Glory Maximisation: The Ressurection of Lazarus.

It is not surprising that Jesus would use the same strategy as Abba Father does, which is to prolong the time in which he performed a miracle so as to reap as much glory out of it as possible. Jesus Christ was simply affirming who He is, the incarnate Christ, God who came as man to redeem the world. Paul the apostle said

"Christ is the visible image of the invisible God. He existed before anything was created and is supreme over all creation..." (Col. 1:15). Jesus himself said *"I and [my] Father are one" (John 10:30 KJV).*

In his ministry, Jesus did only the works or will of the Father as he was instructed. (John 5:17,19, 30) and also spoke only what the Father asked him to speak (John 12:49). Having heard that Lazarus was sick, Jesus did not go to Bethany immediately by the time Jesus arrived, Lazarus had been in the tomb for four days (John 11:17). No one who knew Jesus

had been sent for could understand why he had taken so long to arrive after all he loved Lazarus and his sisters Martha and Mary. Even Mary told Jesus that her brother would have not died if he had come earlier.
Miracles reveal to the unbeliever that God is indeed real and they testify that He sent Jesus Christ. Jesus' goal in his ministry was to glorify God and he chose at this time a strategy God also uses which would bring greater glory to God.

Jesus "stayed where he was two more days,.." (John 11:6) deliberately when he heard that Lazarus was sick because the miracle of resurrecting Lazarus was a far greater glory inducing miracle than healing him would have been. This is why Jesus said when he heard Lazarus was sick "*this sickness is not unto death, but for the glory of God, that the Son of God might be glorified thereby"(John 11:4 KJV).*

We should be encouraged that as God is glorifying himself in all the earth, so he is also performing miracles in our lives and in the lives of our loved ones. There is also a lesson Mary and Martha as well as multitudes must have learnt following the resurrection of Lazarus as well as other miracles of God, which should also serve to assure us God is in absolute control in the worst circumstances. This lesson is that some situations get worse before they get better. As someone, once said "The greater the obstacle, the more the glory in overcoming it".

For Glory Maximisation: The 10 plagues prior to the Exodus.

To the naked eye, Pharaoh was extremely defiant and unreasonable in his reluctance to let God's people go despite several tragic incidents (plagues) which were devastating to the Egyptians and their land. However, when God sent Moses to Pharaoh to demand that he let the Israelites go, God literally spells out what He was going to do and why:

"And the LORD said unto Moses, When thou goest to return into Egypt, see that thou do all those wonders before Pharaoh, which I have put in thine hand: but I will harden his heart, that he shall not let the people go. And thou shalt say unto Pharaoh, Thus saith the LORD, Israel [is] my son, [even] my firstborn. And I say unto thee, Let my son go, that he may serve me: and if thou refuse to let him go, behold, I will slay thy son, [even] thy firstborn." (Exodus 4:21-23 KJV)
"And the LORD hardened the heart of Pharaoh, and he hearkened not unto them; as the LORD had spoken unto Moses." (Exodus 9:12 KJV)
"And I will harden Pharaoh's heart, that he shall follow after them; and I will be honoured upon Pharaoh, and upon all his host; that the Egyptians may know that I [am] the LORD."(Exodus 14: 4 KJV)

The evidence is therefore crystal clear; God allowed Pharaoh to refuse to release the Israelites from bondage each time until after the tenth plague so that

He would, during each of the ten times he sent Moses to Pharaoh, demonstrate His might and power. As a result, the Egyptians suffered the consequences of Pharaoh's hardened heart each time, the tenth and final one was by far the worst in that all the first-born sons of the Egyptians died including Pharaoh's.

The LORD plans to unleash vengeance on our enemies on our behalf and to deliver us from every demonic bondage because as His children and believers in Jesus we are his "first born sons" and so precious to Him.

It is worth noting that before Moses' journey to Egypt when the LORD spoke to him, He mentioned that Pharaoh's hardened heart would result in his first-born son being slain (Ex. 4:23), Moses did not at the time envisage a prolonged nine plagues processes before this most devastating one of death to Egyptian first born sons.

As in this case, the LORD may ask us to do something but He may choose not to give us all the details of the time span, how he would do it or details of some of the joys or dangers and challenges we may encounter along the way but as Moses we must obey nevertheless because our lives or those of multitudes may depend on our obedience. Our obedience as that of Moses did although we may not be conscious of it often has eternal consequences and is for prophetic fulfilment.

Although the Israelites were doubtful and fearful revealed by how their suffering was intensified by Pharaoh at beginning of Moses' demand, he lets them go, the prolonged wait to perform His miracle of deliverance of His people was worth it to God. This is because through it He demonstrated that He was the one and only Almighty, Omnipotent God who Pharaoh, the magicians and gods of Egypt could not withstand or stop.

Our God is in every situation we go through. He sees, knows and cares. What appears to the naked eye or in the natural is often not what the full picture is or how it will remain permanently. In order to have God's perspective of things or understanding of His ways, we must determine to stay as close to Him and Jesus Christ as possible through daily bible study, prayer and praise.

The Holy Spirit is activated as a result and we become ones who walk in the Spirit with the gifts and fruit of the Spirit able to know God and have His wisdom, knowledge and understanding. In addition, whatever the enemy throws at us will never derail us because our soul knows well that in every "storm" or unsettling situation God is at work in His supernatural ways we may not understand for however long it pleases Him to reap as much glory out of it as possible.

Chapter 3
The Leading & Abiding Presence of God

The children of Israel were preparing to enter the Promised Land when they were commanded as follows (Joshua 3:3-4):

1. When they saw the Ark of the Covenant being carried by the Levitical priests, they were to follow it.

2. They were not to follow too closely behind but were to leave "a distance of about 2,000 cubits by measure" between them and the ark. The reason for this distance? So that they may know the way by which they should go for they had not passed that way before.

God told the Israelites to keep a distance between them and the ark so that they would know which way they should go because they had not gone that way before. What instantly springs to mind is this statement: Whether they kept a distance between them and the ark even the exact distance required of them by God or not, the fact remained that they had never passed that way before. So why was it so important for them to keep that distance of "about 2,000 cubits by measure?" When we read and meditate on the Old Testament, we conclude that the

God of Israel revealed Himself in different ways which resulted in the different names by which He was referred to by the Israelites.

His names reveal who He is and how His people saw Him then and do so now. His names also reveal His elevation and exaltation above other gods of false religions. Therefore, while the God of Israel manifests Himself as a personable God who even used emotional words and phrases to express His longing for His people through His prophets, He also presents Himself as One to be revered or as one to whom Israel were expected to have a reverential fear and therefore to ascribe their uttermost respect through worship of Him alone.

In fact, one of the seven Spirits of God (attributes of Christ expressed as seven spirits) mentioned in Isaiah 11, is the (reverential) Fear of the LORD. We must also remember that God is Spirit and those who worship Him must do so in Spirit and in truth. When one is esteemed, it means that their presence and acts of generosity, love and kindness are not taken for granted or disrespected.

The ancient Israelites had been brought up giving God and His presence represented by the Ark of the Covenant placed in the Holy of Holies in the tent of meeting in the wilderness, then later in the Temple, the reverence and respect due them. It is therefore not surprising that they would not think it strange to be told by God to keep a specific distance between them and the Ark of the Covenant.

They knew that their complete obedience was important to God. Many times, in scripture we encounter a God of precision. Even in the building of the tabernacle or tent of meeting in the wilderness, God gave specific instructions and measurements as well as where every item should be placed.

In addition, it was not permissible by God that King Saul during his battle with the Amalekites had killed all of them but spared their king and kept the best of the livestock to use as sacrifice to God. This is because God had instructed King Saul to destroy all the Amalekites including their possessions which included livestock. Saul's partial obedience was still disobedience as the prophet Samuel had told him. The prophet also told King Saul the adverse consequences of his disobedience (1 Samuel 15:22-23).

Obedience to God should not be partial. We must endeavour to obey God completely regardless of the cost which may include mockery by others or loss of reputation. The exact or complete obedience of the Israelites was seen by God as an expression of their love for Him and affirmed that they held Him in the highest esteem as one to be revered or respected above anyone or anything.

In the wilderness journey, the children of Israel suffered the consequences of disobedience to God, some did not make it to the Promised Land because of their disobedience. In return for their absolute obedience, they were led or directed to exactly where God intended His presence (the ark) to take them which was the promised land of Canaan.

NEW COVENANT CONTEXT

The LORD is speaking to us today clearly through this account as New Covenant believers in Jesus Christ. When we are about to start a new undertaking such as a new project or job or to commence a new day or year, we are to liken our preparation as ones preparing to enter into our "promised land". In other words, we should be as the Israelites, expectant to receive our God given inheritance or promise as a result of the "journey" or outworking of whatever we are about to begin or take part in. As children of God, we must trust God that His presence always goes before us in whatever we do, always praying:
"*Shew me thy ways, O LORD; teach me thy paths Lead me in thy truth, and teach me for thou [art] the God of my salvation; on thee do I wait all the day.(Ps. 25:4-5 KJV).*

We have a great High Priest Jesus Christ seated at the Right Hand of God making intercession for us. He also left us with the Holy Spirit who indwells every true believer in Jesus Christ and is also our intercessor and enables us to know God and His will for our lives.

In order to "*see the Ark of Covenant and be positioned in the direction the priests are taking it*" or to abide in the presence of God through Jesus Christ and the Holy Spirit, God requires our absolute or complete obedience. Our God has not changed from ancient times in terms of His fundamental requirements and principles.

As the ancient Israelites expressed their love for God through complete obedience to God's command by remaining a certain distance away from the Ark when following it, and in other ways we read in the Old Testament, so too we express our love to Jesus (who is one with God; John 10:30) by obeying his commands as he said:
"*He that hath my commandments, and keepeth them, he it is that loveth me: and he that loveth me shall be loved of my Father, and I will love him, and will manifest myself to him....Jesus answered and said unto him, If a man love me, he will keep my words: and my Father will love him, and we will come unto him, and make our abode with him. (John 14:21,23* KJV)

The rewards of our obedience are also clear from these verses;
Father God will love us and both He and Jesus will come and make their home with us. This is a clear indication that the fundamental key to abiding in God's presence is obeying the Word of God in its entirety; if we obey Jesus' commands we are doing so, because He is the Word of God personified (John 1:1-5,14).

In His presence we receive His joy (Ps. 16:11), His protection (Ps.91) and the ability to see our way forward for we gain revelation and insight into His will, plans and purposes for our lives and are able to help others as well. In His presence therefore we are God's true brides immersed in His love through Jesus Christ our bridegroom. A relationship of everlasting love is sustained by our obedience which in itself speaks of our reverence and respect of God and Christ so that we give them the highest place in our hearts.

"Keep thy heart with all diligence; for out of it are the issues of life (Prov.4:23KJV).

Brethren, the heart of man can be deceitful even when we are saved as Satan never gives up on us! Therefore, in order to ensure we are led and guided by God daily and at the beginning of every undertaking, we must constantly guard our hearts and minds so as to sustain a life in the Fear of the LORD and in His presence. This can only be possible if we do so in exactly the way He requires as to, exact obedience with reverence that is, so that the idiom "familiarity breeds contempt" does not in any way manifest, even subconsciously, in the way we treat or relate to our God and our Lord Jesus Christ. Brethren let us have this mindset and it shall be well with us.

Chapter 4
Enter the Treasure Door of God's Wisdom

"Forsake her not, and she shall preserve thee: love her, and she shall keep thee. Wisdom is the principal thing; therefore get wisdom: and with all thy getting get understanding. Exalt her, and she shall promote thee: she shall bring thee to honour, when thou dost embrace her. She shall give to thine head an ornament of grace: a crown of glory shall she deliver to thee." (Proverbs 4:6-9 KJV).

"If thou seekest her as silver, and searchest for her as for hid treasures; Then shalt thou understand the fear of the LORD and find the knowledge of God."(Proverbs 2:4-5 KJV).

Here are some of the definitions of the word wisdom from dictionaries but expressed in the context of God's wisdom. Through Father God, we have
-insight or the ability to discern or judge what is true, right, or lasting. (thefreedictionary.com)
-have experience, knowledge, and good judgement; the quality of being wise (oxforddictionaries.com).

In summary, God's wisdom speaks of God's ways that are true and righteous and express who He is. It is only when we understand God's ways (insight into His truth, knowledge, judgement etc...) that we know why He acts the way He does. This is why wisdom and understanding are as Siamese twins, fused together as one and cannot exist without the other.

"Happy is the man that findeth wisdom, and the man that getteth understanding. For the merchandise of it is better than the merchandise of silver, and the gain thereof than fine gold. She is more precious than rubies: and all the things thou canst desire are not to be compared unto her." (Prov. 3:13-15 KJV).

Gold and silver are precious metals, but they are not as valuable as the Wisdom and understanding of God. It is not enough reading our bible, we must understand the purpose for which it exists and most important of all we must know the author, the Most High God and the fact that He is to be revered. To gain the wisdom of God, which encompasses knowledge and brings about understanding of His ways, we must be in constant fellowship with the Holy Spirit, who is the Spirit of prophecy and Testimony of Jesus (Rev. 19:10).

Among the attributes of the Holy Spirit, which are the nature of Christ expressed as seven spirits of God, are the spirit of wisdom, understanding and knowledge. (Isaiah 11:2).
Jesus in the Apostle Paul's words is Wisdom personified (1 Corinth. 1:30). He also says that Jesus is God's wisdom (1 Corinth. 1:23-24). We also know that Jesus personifies the Word of God through which we obtain God's wisdom (John 1:1-

5).Without constant reminder of the teachings of Jesus by the Holy Spirit (John 14:26) we would not be able to have the wisdom of God, for this reason we should be thankful that Jesus prayed to the Father to send his disciples the Holy Spirit. The Holy Spirit enables us to live a life abiding in Christ through Christ. These verses express this so well:

"Howbeit we speak wisdom among them that are perfect: yet not the wisdom of this world, nor of the princes of this world, that come to nought: But we speak the wisdom of God in a mystery, even the hidden wisdom, which God ordained before the world unto our glory: Which none of the princes of this world knew: for had they known it, they would not have crucified the LORD of glory.
But as it is written, Eye hath not seen, nor ear heard, neither have entered into the heart of man, the things which God hath prepared for them that love him.

But God hath revealed them unto us by his Spirit: for the Spirit searcheth all things, yea, the deep things of God. For what man knoweth the things of a man, save the spirit of man which is in him? even so the things of God knoweth no man, but the Spirit of God. Now we have received, not the spirit of the world, but the spirit which is of God; that we might know the things that are freely given to us of God.

Which things also we speak, not in the words which man's wisdom teacheth, but which the Holy Ghost teacheth; comparing spiritual things with spiritual.

But the natural man receiveth not the things of the Spirit of God: for they are foolishness unto him: neither can he know them, because they are spiritually discerned. But he that is spiritual judgeth all things, yet he himself is judged of no man.For who hath known the mind of the LORD, that he may instruct him? but we have the mind of Christ." (1 Corinth. 2:6-16 KJV).

In summary, Paul states that the apostles are inspired to speak God's wisdom by the Spirit of God who knows and reveals the mind of God concerning the things that He has for those that love Him. The wisdom that is demonstrated by envy, strife and deceit which reaps confusion, and every evil work is "earthly, sensual, devilish" according to James 3:16 (KJV). But the wisdom that we must seek is from God and *"is first pure, then peaceable, gentle and easy to be intreated, full of mercy and good fruits, without partiality, and without hypocrisy."(James 3:17KJV).*

There is a mystery and preciousness attached to God's wisdom so that it is referred to as "hidden treasure" (Prov. 2:4) or "wisdom of God in a mystery, even the hidden wisdom, which God ordained before the world unto our glory" (1 Corinth. 2:7). The fact that it is hidden or mysterious gives us the understanding that it must be sought with effort in order to be found. Only a select few who are willing to seek or search for it sacrificially and with fervor will attain God's wisdom although it is available to all. Such people are those who

1) Make it a habit to constantly call on God:
Jeremiah 33:3: *Call on me and I will show you*
-Great and mighty things (King James Version) or
-Remarkable secrets (New Living Translation) or
-Great and unsearchable things (New International Version) or
-Great & Mysterious things (NET bible)
you do not know.

2) Study the Word of God diligently because they care about pleasing the LORD and handling or teaching the word truthfully. (2 Timothy 2:15).

3) As believers in Jesus Christ seek the Kingdom of God with all their heart sacrificially:
44 "The Kingdom of Heaven is like a treasure that a man discovered hidden in a field. In his excitement, he hid it again and sold everything he owned to get enough money to buy the field. (Matt.13:44 NIV).

When we seek first the precious kingdom of God and His righteousness, Jesus said all things will be added to us (Matthew 6:33).
We must examine our hearts and ask ourselves whether we are among the few who are willing to seek or search for God's wisdom day and night so that we can take hold of all that God has promised those who love Him. It is evident that we lose out on the immense riches of God's wisdom if we do not develop such a lifestyle. We must be determined

to be devoted to God wholeheartedly and constantly seek His wisdom and encourage others to do the same.

Gracious Father,
thank you for the wisdom we have through Christ Jesus and the Holy Spirit who abides in and with those who love you. Forgive us when we have made our own judgements, walked our own way and attempted to help you in fulfilling our destinies.

We pray for an increase in your wisdom, knowledge and understanding in our lives and that we would be ones who daily speak words and walk in your wisdom, under the inspiration of your Holy Spirit. Help us LORD, for our desire is to be a blessing to our brethren in the church and others in the world. In Jesus' mighty name, we pray, Amen.

Chapter 5
God fulfils His Prophetic Word & Answers Prayers

Part 1 God will bring His words to pass his way!

I don't know what you are waiting on the LORD for, but I have a message for you today: I sense the LORD is saying continue abiding in Him, trusting Him and He will bring it to pass His way.

"I have spoken it, I will bring it to pass" (Isaiah 46:11).

In 1994 I sensed the LORD saying that He has called me to "write and bear witness" of Him, six years later in the year 2000 at a prophetic conference one of the prophets prophesied that God has called me to write, He will give me what to write and that I will write many books. I praise God that I am walking fully in this prophetic word.

Therefore, whether the prophetic word was given directly to you, through a world renowned or seasoned prophet or a fellow believer in Christ who hears from God, it will surely come to pass. Our God cannot lie, and His Word is life giving, transforming and sets in motion as well as propels His children forward into the fulfilment of His predestined plans.

As we know God does not speak for the sake of speaking; God's Word whether the written Word (Bible) or spoken prophetic Word is *"Alive and Active"* (Heb. 4:12) and is therefore bound to bear fruit or be productive for His glory.

These two scriptures among others illustrate this point very well:
1 Samuel 3:19 - God did not let any of the words He spoke through the prophet Samuel go unfulfilled in his lifetime.

Isaiah 55:10-11 – 10 *“The rain and snow come down from the heavens and stay on the ground to water the earth. They cause the grain to grow, producing seed for the farmer and bread for the hungry. 11 It is the same with my word I send it out, and it always produces fruit. It will accomplish all I want it to, and it will prosper everywhere I send it.” (NLT).*

So dear Brethren, let us always be expectant with joy in relation to what God has in store for us. We may know only some of His plans for us personally but there is much more;
"No eye has seen, no ear has heard, and no mind has imagined what God has prepared for those who love him." (1 Corinthians 2:9NLT).

In addition, the Bible is full of promises for God's children; it is time to consciously receive them by

faith and declare them over our personal lives if we are not doing so already.
Be encouraged! "You shall live in Joy and Peace...". (Is. 55:12).

Part 2 Prayers avail much, God's way.

God's Word to you today, you who pray and praise him ceaselessly, is that before you asked Him anything in prayer, He knew you would because He knows you and all your desires. This may be stating the obvious, but we often tend to forget.

Therefore do not be discouraged if your prayers do not get answered immediately as in the case of Hannah when she prayed and sobbed continuously before the LORD for a child. It took a while, but she persevered and did not give up. So don't give up on the LORD as He never gives up on you. What you are seeking from the LORD could be His divine will such as in the case of Hannah.

Even before Hannah travailed in prayer, the LORD had planned to give her a child. Her son was not only given to her for her pleasure but also for the sake of God's people, Israel. This is because at the time the Word of the LORD was scarce, in other words, God could hardly find anyone through whom He could speak. Also the priests were corrupt. Samuel, Hannah's son was predestined to be the prophet and priest Israel needed at the time.

Even before Paul and Silas prayed and sang hymns to Him while in prison (Acts 16) and the church prayed ceaselessly for Peter (Acts 12) while he was in prison, God had declared these men would be freed. The miracle of breakage of chains and release of Paul and Silas as well as other prisoners was heard by many and involved the salvation of the prison guard, so their prayers and praise resulted in testimonies and salvation to the glory of God.

Do not underestimate the power of your prayers and praise to affect individuals, families, communities, and nations. Do not stop! Someone’s healing or their salvation and a nations’ restoration could depend on your praise and prayers as the LORD may have commissioned you alone or you among others to be His instrument.

This is why the apostle Paul encouraged the church to *"Rejoice evermore. Pray without ceasing. In everything give thanks: for this is the will of God in Christ Jesus concerning you." (1 Thess.5: 16-18)*

If you are praying for something that may not be God's will for you, He is merciful and gracious and will honour you because you sought Him in the first instance. He will instead outwork what He has predestined for you although it was not exactly what you prayed for. The fact is that He created you so as your Heavenly Father He knows even better than you what is good for you.

There may be several reasons why your prayers may appear to be taking forever to get answers, but here are two:

1. God is molding you into the type of person who would be ready for what you are praying for. Perhaps you are praying for marriage or your church or ministry to grow. The question is are you ready spiritually, emotionally or with the necessary skills and knowledge? You may think you know, but only He knows the reality of whether you are ready or not.
2. God has planned an appointed time for you to have what you have been praying for in the way in which he knows is best for you. This is because certain things have to happen in the wider scheme of things before your specific prayer is answered or answering your prayer is part of a chain of events that must happen at the same time.

God is sovereign and can choose to do things this way.

"But, beloved, be not ignorant of this one thing, that one day is with the LORD as a thousand years, and a thousand years as one day." (2 Peter 3:8 KJV).

What may appear as delay to you is God's perfect timing. The manifestation is likely to come when you least expect it. Meanwhile as you wait for God to answer your prayer, pray not just for what you want on a superficial level, rather tell the LORD how you will be committed to Him through whatever you are asking Him for or how it would help you glorify Him more. Hannah for instance made a vow that she would offer her child to the LORD, and she fulfilled her vow (1 Samuel 1:11/22).

Even if it is a prayer for someone else, the testimony of that person's breakthrough is something you can promise God that you will share on that person's behalf to the glory of God. If you are praying for your own healing or that of someone else, present God's Word before Him by quoting what He says about His will to heal all sicknesses and diseases. Pray for your future spouse in detail if you are praying for marriage, God knows who they are and when they will be ready for marriage. As we pray, it is important to be aware of the power of the Holy Spirit in prayer, for He intercedes for us according to the will of Father as we often do not know what or how to pray.

Therefore brothers and sisters let us rejoice, be thankful in everything as we wait in prayer for all that God has planned for us because our Heavenly Father only wants what is best for us and will bring it to pass according to His perfect will in His perfect time.

Chapter 6
God's timing is Perfect

Part 1 In the fullness of time, "...Thy kingdom come, thy will be done..."

Everything that is dropped from above inevitably falls to the ground, right? This is the law of gravity and is no doubt one of God's natural laws. Likewise, there are other laws and principles governing nature and how things happen in our Christian lives which are consistent or unchanging. I will put it simply in this manner:

Everything comes to full term, and there is always an appointed time for everything.
"When the fullness of the time was come, God sent forth his Son, made of a woman, made under the law, to redeem them that were under the law, that we might receive the adoption of sons. And because ye are sons, God hath sent forth the Spirit of his Son into your hearts, crying, Abba, Father. Wherefore thou art no more a servant, but a son; and if a son, then an heir of God through Christ." (Gal 4:4-7 KJV).

"To every [thing there is] a season, and a time to every purpose under the heaven: A time to be born, and a time to die; a time to plant, and a time to pluck up [that which is] planted..." (Ecc. 3:1-2 KJV).

A mother who conceives carries her child and brings the child forth in the time God planned, often it is nine months, but at times a few months less or some days more.

We fix our eyes on Jesus who is not only the "author" but also the "finisher of our Faith" (Heb.12:2). The Word of God is spoken of as accomplishing the purpose for which it was sent in likeness to the rains that come down (Is.55:10-11).

In Isaiah 66:7-14, Jerusalem's bringing forth a male child in a day and the wonders thereafter to the glory of God are a cause for joy:

"7Before she travailed, she brought forth; before her pain came, she was delivered of a man child.8Who hath heard such a thing? who hath seen such things? Shall the earth be made to bring forth in one day? [or] shall a nation be born at once? for as soon as Zion travailed, she brought forth her children.9Shall I bring to the birth, and not cause to bring forth? saith the LORD: shall I cause to bring forth, and shut [the womb]? saith thy God.10Rejoice ye with Jerusalem, and be glad with her, all ye that love her: rejoice for joy with her, all ye that mourn for her:

11That ye may suck, and be satisfied with the breasts of her consolations; that ye may milk out, and be delighted with the abundance of her glory.12For thus saith the LORD, Behold, I will extend peace to her like a river, and the glory of the Gentiles like a flowing stream: then shall ye suck, ye shall be borne upon [her] sides, and be dandled upon [her] knees.13As one whom his mother comforteth, so will I comfort you; and ye shall be comforted in Jerusalem.14And when ye see [this], your heart shall rejoice, and your bones shall flourish like an herb: and the hand of the LORD shall be known toward his servants, and [his] indignation toward his enemies." (Is. 66:7-14 KJV)

Even before Jerusalem where King David had his throne, (the capital city of Israel at the time and where the Apostolic church of the first century by Jesus' disciples was founded) "travailed" or laboured, she is said to have already fulfilled her destiny? What does this mean?

This means the "man child" our Lord Jesus Christ referred to in Is. 66:7, existed well before Jerusalem itself. He is one with God, the world was created by him, for him and through him (Col 1:16). It was God's plan that Jerusalem, here representing Israel was a whole will bring forth the "man child". Jesus Christ, the King of God's kingdom will be born in Judea the province where Jerusalem was.

Thus because it was a decree of God almighty established before the foundations of the earth, before Jerusalem and the people associated with her would travail (Isaiah was prophesying a future occurrence) through pain and hardships for the fulfilment of God's plans, these plans were decreed already fulfilled in the earth realm; As we read later verses of Isaiah 66, we gain the understanding that the coming of Jesus Christ shall result in multitudes of conversions and therefore transformed lives of Israelites as well as Gentiles who will go to Jerusalem. God's people will then be sent from there, Jerusalem itself and one discerns it also means the church of Jesus Christ in the nations of the world (being a type of Jerusalem, the "Holy Mountain") to other places around the world. Praise the LORD! No wonder Isaiah is referred to as the Salvation prophet!

Jerusalem is personified and depicted as a mother breast feeding her children and carrying them in her arms. It is also shown through Isaiah as a place where God promises "peace like a river" and that He would show His indignation against God's enemies for the sake of His people. Jerusalem fulfilled her God given destiny over the centuries in a process mingled with heartache or suffering and joy. There is more to come.

Does that ring a bell? In our lives as believers in Jesus Christ, the journey to fulfil our God given destiny involves travail through pain or afflictions but there are also joyful moments, praise the LORD! Let us be encouraged that as Jerusalem, even before we travail or suffer for the purposes of God to be fulfilled in our life through Christ, we are decreed victorious because those purposes are God's established predestined plans in heaven.

This is why Jesus taught his disciples to pray by including the line *"Thy kingdom come, thy will be done on earth as it is in heaven" (Matt. 6:10)*. As we keep on being a source of nurturing for others in true godliness and allowing God to birth the righteousness of the "man child" through our thoughts and deeds we must rejoice for our destiny as planned by God is unfolding according to His perfect will. In addition, we are to rest assured that whatever we are expecting from God such as answers to prayers or His prophetic promises will surely come to pass in His appointed time.

Often, we say "when Lord will this happen? I have been waiting so long!" The time of preparation or the gestation period for birthing specific plans is important for our spiritual development and maturity and God knows what we will need in the process which will glorify Him as much as when we obtain what we have been waiting for.

God is faithful to bring to pass what He promises: *"Shall I bring to the birth, and not cause to bring forth? saith the LORD: shall I cause to bring forth and shut the womb (Is. 66:9).* In addition, Jerusalem or Zion brought forth her children, "as soon as she travailed" or in "one day", this impresses upon us the sudden appearance of God's plans and purposes.

Likewise following the process of travail, when we finally receive what we have travailed for to the glory of God, it often appears as a sudden occurrence! In fact, we often do not know God's timing for His promises to manifest in our lives. The anticipation of sudden happenings is one of the most exciting aspects of our Christian walk!

Jerusalem's testimony among others should be an encouragement to us that come what may, rain or shine, in pain or joy, God's plans always come to pass so we say humbly: "we will wait patiently on you, LORD".

Part 2 The power & timing of God's ideas.

"There is nothing more powerful than an idea whose time has come!" Victor Hugo

I see this quote as having more depth and meaning in a Christian context. This scripture comes to mind: "*But when the fulness of the time was come, God sent forth his Son, made of a woman, made under the law,*[5] *To redeem them that were under the law, that we might receive the adoption of sons." (Galatians 4:4-5 KJV).*

Sending Jesus Christ was God's great and powerful idea at His perfect timing. In fact, He came to earth in the person of Jesus Christ (John 10:30)

God was in Christ, reconciling the world unto himself, not imputing their trespasses unto them; and hath committed unto us the word of

reconciliation.” (2 Corinthians 5:19 KJV).

This is how God took back His possession. Yes, you and I!

A Man of War, (Jehovah Gibbor) through this idea came to fight a battle on behalf of mankind and took us from the clutches of Satan by redeeming us from our sins.
How awesome!
How touching!

Yes, God came as man in the flesh to reconcile the world back to Himself. His ideas are incomparable in greatest to those of human beings, the created. What a genius is our God, the greatest of all!

God has many powerful ideas that manifest as plans for you and I attainable through Christ and in God’s appointed time.

Yes, at different times during our life He brings them to fruition, they germinate from seed, emerge as stems with leaves, flowers and fruit ready for the picking and fragranced with heavenly scents that bring healing and restoration to us and those we encounter. God's ideas are no small thing for they are simultaneously for individual, family, community, national and world transformation.

So you see God's ideas are powerful and indeed exert unmatchable power when their time of unravelling comes!

In scripture we read about all the powerful work that Jesus did. He went about doing good, healing the sick, casting out demons and giving hope to the hopeless. Jesus read about his mission from the book of Isaiah Chapter 61:

"The Spirit of the LORD is upon me, because he hath anointed me to preach the gospel to the poor; he hath sent me to heal the brokenhearted, to preach deliverance to the captives, and recovering of sight to the blind, to set at liberty them that are bruised, To preach the acceptable year of the LORD" (Luke 4:18-19 KJV).

We also read the following account from the book of Acts:

"How God anointed Jesus of Nazareth with the Holy Ghost and with power: who went about doing good, and healing all that were oppressed of the devil; for God was with him." (Acts 10:38 KJV).

God has multitude ideas for us. Are you seeking Him daily and fervently to know what God's ideas or plans are for you? He said to Israel and He says to New Covenant believers as well:

"For I know the thoughts that I think toward you, saith the LORD, thoughts of peace, and not of evil, to give you an expected end." (Jer.29:11 KJV)

It is never too late to be a diligent seeker of God's ideas or plans. God is patient and a redeemer of time lost as other things. He is a God of second chances.

While we partner with God to outwork His plans in our lives, through us God's powerful creativity manifests as whatever He does in our lives with and through us reflects His awesome creative power. So, what are you waiting for? Indeed, the set time is now! Have an exciting era of discovery and recovery of God's powerful ideas.

Chapter 7
God Tests & Chastens His People

Part 1 God chastens & tests us for his purposes.

God chastens those He loves (Hebrews 12:6). He can allow affliction to happen in our lives for some time for the purpose of chastening us. God knows how much we can handle and will not allow us to suffer beyond what we can bear (1 Corinth. 10:13).

To chasten means to
- correct by punishment or suffering.
- have a restraining or moderating effect on.

The Holy Spirit as the power of God can manifest as the consuming fire of God to convict us when we sin for the purpose of refining us. When our sins are highlighted by God's supernatural grace, we have a choice to make; will we acknowledge and confess them before the LORD and ask those we have wronged for forgiveness or ignore the Holy Spirit's prompting which is for the purpose of cleansing us from all unrighteousness (1 John 1:9)? To get our attention, sometimes God will allow suffering.

When the Israelites were in the wilderness, Moses said to them, "He [God] gave you manna to eat in the wilderness, something your ancestral had never known, to humble and to test you so that it might go well with you" (Deut. 8:16). God could have given the children of Israel the type of bread or food they were familiar with, but He chose to give them manna, the miraculous "bread of heaven", a small round substance which tasted like nothing they had ever eaten before (Ps. 78:24, Ex. 16:14,31).

At times the LORD will allow us into territories or places we are unfamiliar with or undergo experiences we have never undergone before for the purpose of humbling and testing us, so that "it might go well with us" (Deut.8:16).

If you have something so precious to you, will you be willing to give it away if God asks you to? Abraham was tested after God gave him Isaac, his much-awaited son. God told him to kill Isaac and Abraham did not hesitate, he went ahead to make the preparations. God however stopped Abraham just before he killed Isaac and provided a ram to replace him. As a result of Abraham's obedience, God's covenant blessings to him and his descendants were confirmed by God (Gen. 22:1-18).

This ought to encourage us to surrender all to the LORD sacrificially, because His principles are to reward those who diligently seek Him and to cause us to reap what we sow for His sake. God is always searching for those who will make a choice to be fully committed to Him regardless of the circumstances, in other words in good times or in times of hardship or affliction. Being fully committed to the LORD means allowing chastening and being quick to acknowledge and confess our sins. In addition, we are willing to live sacrificially or forgo what pleases us for what pleases God.

My prayer is that we will respond daily to God's plans to humble and test us so that it will always be well with us. Dear brothers and sisters, let us also remember the apostle James' counsel to us:

"Count it all joy, my brothers when you fall into various temptations, knowing that the testing of your faith produces endurance. Let endurance have its perfect work, that you may be perfect and complete, lacking in nothing" (James 1:2-4 KJV).

Part 2 Want the next stage of a blessed promise or promotion? Be prepared to be tested by God.

Job & Abraham's use of the master "key": Obedience

When God is about to bless you greatly, promote you or take you to the next level of a blessed promise, brethren, He will test you. You may say "but I don't know what constitutes a test or a mere call to be obedient".

My response is "Well then it is best to be obedient all the time so as not to miss that which God would bring your way prior to Him blessing, promoting you or bringing about a breakthrough in your life".

I was thinking of all this when I read "*When Job prayed for his friends, the LORD restored his fortunes. In fact, the LORD gave him twice as much as before!* " *(Job 42:10 NLT)*.

Note the word "When" at the beginning of the verse meaning it was after Job prayed for His friends that God did what He had planned to do, which was to recompense or restore to Job twice as much as he had before. One would say "but wait a minute, Job had suffered so much, and it is not fair that praying for his friends was a condition for him to be doubly blessed!"

Another similar situation comes to mind. Abraham and Sarah had been promised a child by God. When they had Isaac their sought-after child at God's appointed time, lo and behold God told Abraham to sacrifice Isaac as one would an animal. In our natural mind that does not make sense!

The immediate reaction could be the following "Why would God want Abraham to do that! Ishmael who was not the promised child of God did not have that fate, so why Isaac!" But Abraham as in the case of Job did not protest instead, he obeyed God wholeheartedly. The bible clearly states that God tested Abraham (Genesis 22:1). When Abraham obeyed God and was about to lift the knife to kill his son Isaac who was lying on the altar, this is what happened:

"..the angel of the LORD called unto him out of heaven, and said, Abraham, Abraham: and he said, Here [am] I. and he said Lay not thine hand upon the lad, neither do thou anything unto him: for now I know that thou fearest God, seeing thou hast not withheld thy son, thine only [son] from me." (Gen. 22:11-12 KJV).

In Abraham's case as in the case of Job, we are given the understanding that after obedience, a blessing promised is declared affirmed as unlocked or loose in the earth realm by God.

The act of obedience is the KEY that unlocks the intended blessing. It will remain an unrealised promise until one passes the test of obedience.
These two examples of Job and Abraham are examples of God's ways. How God will test his people in a specific manner and his ultimate decision as to whether to release a blessing or not will depend on their response. The God of the Old Testament is the same God that we serve through our Lord and Saviour Jesus Christ and his principles and ways have not changed.

I wrote earlier that "after obedience, a blessing promised is declared affirmed as unlocked or loose in the earth realm."

"I will give unto thee the keys of the kingdom of heaven: and whatsoever thou shalt bind on earth shall be bound in heaven: and whatsoever thou shalt

loose on earth shall be loosed in heaven." (Matt.16:19 KJV).

Anyone who confesses that Jesus is *"the Christ, Son of the living God" (Matt. 16:16)* as Simon Peter, Jesus' disciple did, has received this revelation from Father God (Matt. 16:17) and is promised the power and authority through partnering with God to bring manifested change in the earth realm from heaven according to Matthew 16:19. This is the promise to all Christians.

Therefore, many believers think of "binding and loosing" in terms of proclaiming or verbalising in spiritual warfare prayers what they believe to be true: that Satan is bound, and God's promises are loose for their sake. It is not wrong to do this, but my message is this, brethren always have at the forefront of your minds this truth: that Satan and his demons are bound in your life and God's promises are loose in your life by virtue of your obedience to God!

When Jesus spoke in the manner quoted in Matthew 16:19, it was said to his disciples then and those who will become his disciples. There is an expectation by Jesus that his disciples would be obedient because this is a requirement of being one of Jesus' disciples. What does obedience do?

It demonstrates that there is a love for Christ and the reward is God's love and presence manifesting in the disciple's life as according to John 14:21, 23. We can only do the works and greater works of God (John

14:12) as promised by Christ, if we activate the authority we have in Jesus Christ who said *"I will give unto thee the keys of the kingdom of heaven: and whatsoever thou shalt bind on earth shall be bound in heaven: and whatsoever thou shalt loose on earth shall be loosed in heaven".(Matthew 16:19 KJV).*

When he said this, Jesus was saying "You have my delegated authority, use it to do my works and greater works in the power of the Holy Spirit. However, the degree of our obedience to God as Christians determines the degree in which we remain in God's presence and are anointed to do Jesus' works and even greater works as he promised we would (John 14:12). Obedience is therefore important if we want our binding and losing to fulfil the purpose for which Jesus intended it to. When we are obedient to God and Christ, all of God's promises or blessings which include provision, protection and peace are at our disposal.

This is a much better option than partial obedience which opens one's life to demonic attack and presence. The result being that one feels the need to sweat or strive constantly in spiritual warfare prayers of binding and loosing as one lacks God's peace and discerns that there is something wrong. When we decide to obey God wholeheartedly every day and do all that is humanly possible to do so, God helps us, and we experience His constant presence through which we receive His protection, provision and peace that surpasses all understanding.

God's ways are not man's ways. The wisdom of God is foolishness to man. Man cannot in his natural mind understand the wisdom of God most of the time. Let us remember that the act of praying for friends especially as in Job's case, those that discourage us or say hurtful things to us, is part of the requirement of a God of relationship for His people.

This act of forgiveness comes under the command in the Old Covenant by God that His people are to love Him (Deut. 6:4-5) as well as love their neighbours as themselves (Lev. 19:18). Jesus commanded the same, two greatest commandments for New Covenant believers (Matthew 22:36-40).
In the following verses during Jesus' teachings, we deduce who our "neighbours" include in God's perspective:

"43 Ye have heard that it hath been said, Thou shalt love thy neighbour, and hate thine enemy.
44 But I say unto you, Love your enemies, bless them that curse you, do good to them that hate you, and pray for them which despitefully use you, and persecute you;" (Matt. 5:43-44 KJV).

Our neighbour in the context of Leviticus 19 or Matthew 22 is according to God, our fellow human being regardless of who they are or how they treat us. So, we see that even though Job's friends were not exactly friendly in their discourse with him in his time of deep sorrow, God still expected Job to love them and demonstrate this love by forgiving them and praying for them.

Forgiveness is not easy, but it is a command from God that if obeyed, is a great key, one of many that is activated by the Master key of obedience. It is a great key that enables us
to be blessed by God or receive his promises and answers to our prayers. This is because it first and foremost allows us to make peace with God, which means His favour is restored in our lives.

This in turn results in our own sins being forgiven (Matthew 6:12, 14-15) because God only forgives us our sins if we forgive those who have sinned against us. When we are forgiven by God all that God has planned for us, including answers to prayers begin to manifest.

May we be obedient to God always and be highly sensitive to his promptings to do what may be unusual or appear unreasonable to mankind. This is because these acts are likely to be tests that if passed will result in us entering a more productive stage of our destiny as according to the predestined plan of God.

Chapter 8
God Uses the Enemies of His People for His purposes.

Part 1 Your enemies are mere "Clubs" or "Tools" in God's hand.

God allows afflictions in the lives of those He loves as a form of judgment for the purpose of Chastening us. This is how He also dealt with the children of Israel in biblical time.

This is how God spoke through the prophet Isaiah about Assyria as his instrument of afflict against Israel:

5 "What sorrow awaits Assyria, the rod of my anger.
I use it as a club to express my anger.
6I am sending Assyria against a godless nation,
against a people with whom I am angry.
Assyria will plunder them,
trampling them like dirt beneath its feet. (Isaiah 10:5-6 NLT)

This is one of several references in scripture in which God speaks of using the wicked leader or nation to punish His people, the Israelites.

Those who are used by God to afflict His people are expressed by God as His instruments. For instance Assyria was used by God (Isaiah 10) as His "club" (verse 5) or "tool" to express his anger against Israel.

I am reminded of Judas one of Jesus' twelve disciples, who was a “club” or a “tool” in God's hand to betray Jesus. This happened at the appointed time of God when He allowed Satan to enter Judas so that he went to the religious leaders to discuss how he would betray Jesus in exchange for money which the religious leaders agreed to (Matt.26:14-16). This led to Jesus’ capture and crucifixion.

When agents of Satan are used by God against His own people, these agents as their master Satan are confident that they have God's people bound and under their control whereas in fact they are puppets in God's hands.

This is how God puts it in reference to the King of Assyria:

7But the king of Assyria will not understand that he is my tool;
his mind does not work that way.
His plan is simply to destroy,
to cut down nation after nation.
8He will say,
‘Each of my princes will soon be a king.
9We destroyed Calno just as we did Carchemish.
Hamath fell before us as Arpad did.
And we destroyed Samaria just as we did Damascus.

10Yes, we have finished off many a kingdom
whose gods were greater than those in Jerusalem
and Samaria.
11So we will defeat Jerusalem and her gods,
just as we destroyed Samaria with hers.’” (Isaiah
10:7-11).

Similarly, Satan through Judas' betrayal and the resulting consequences gleefully thought that he had put a stop to Jesus' ministry and purpose forever.

However in scripture we read how Jesus' betrayal and crucifixion were part of God's plan for the purpose of man's redemption and reconciliation to God. This expresses the “mysterious and hidden wisdom of God, which He destined for our glory before time began” that the apostle Paul spoke of in 1 Corinthians 2:7. Paul also said that if the rulers of that age who condoned and strategized for Jesus to be crucified Jesus’ had understood this “mysterious and hidden wisdom of God”, “they would not have crucified the LORD of glory (Jesus)” (1 Corinth 2:7-8 KJV). Indeed, Satan was also unaware that the very plan of Jesus’ crucifixion he instigated through Judas and the religious leaders were allowed by God for His ultimate redemptive purposes. God in His sovereignty always has the final word.

Judas and the king of Assyria are "tools" or instruments of destruction and offense used by God for his purposes because they were wicked men. They lived their lives that way. The king of Assyria at the time and earlier kings as well as later ones are known to have led conquering escapades against nations. The Assyrians worshipped idols and were therefore ungodly. Scripture mentions that Judas was a thief and was known to steal from the disciples' money bag which he oversaw. (John 12:6/John 13:27-29). Although Judas was a Jew, he had no fear of the God of Israel.

Anyone who chooses to live their lives worshipping idols, other gods or in deception rather than as a worshipper of the one and only true God allows themselves to be an instrument of Satan to carry out his plans and purposes. This type of person is not always an obvious enemy of God as in the case of Judah who was in everyone's eyes a loyal disciple of Jesus, following him from town to village as he taught, healed the sick and cast out demons. Such a person whether a child of God or not is motivated to carry out Satan's plans for the purpose of serving as an obstacle or offense to the child of God. They no doubt think they are succeeding as the outcome of their wickedness becomes evident.

Any believer in Christ who does not consciously live to please God even though they may profess to doing so is an easy target of Satan as he roams about the earth seeking people to use to fulfil his plans and purposes (1 Peter 5:8). True Christians must never be complacent as Satan never gives up on them. The reality though, in relation only to children of the God of our Lord Jesus Christ is this: Satan directly or through his agents becomes a club or a tool in God's hand to gauge and control how much evil and suffering is dealt to the believer in Christ and for how long, if indeed God chooses to use their suffering at Satan's hands as a means of punishment or righteous judgement so as to chasten them.

This is because God's children are promised protection and the restoration of their predestined identities and destinies in God. God will therefore apply His grace through Christ's finished work on the cross to ensure His people overcome. The plans or schemes of Satan are counteracted or thwarted for the plans and purposes of God;

"The LORD bringeth the counsel of the heathen to nought: he maketh the devices of the people of none effect. The counsel of the LORD standeth for ever, the thoughts of his heart to all generations. Blessed is the nation whose God is the LORD; and the people whom he hath chosen for his own inheritance. (Psalm 33:10-12 KJV).

However God does not thwart the plans of the enemy without His people playing their part; God's people are required by God to surrender their will and obedience to God so as to activate and sustain this process of breakthrough from the shackles of the enemy. This should encourage those of us who do our best to abide in Him in total surrender. Our partnership with God results in the manifestation of His promise to protect and bless His people.

The enemy may be planning something against us which we do not know about. We may suspect something is amiss, but we know we are powerless to be anything about it.
God can choose to instantly thwart the plan of the enemy or put an end to the affliction we are going through or use it as a means of righteous judgement or punishment to chasten us so that we would be convicted by the Holy Spirit, repent, and turn from our wicked or evil ways. Either way as long as we are children of God, we are more than conquerors and overcomers through Christ who loves us (Romans 8:37) and has overcome the world (John 16:33).

The truth is that Satan cannot afflict a true child of God unless God allows it. God will never allow his children to suffer more than they can take. Why? Because God will literally provide a way of escape and while one is going through it, His strength in the time of suffering will enable one to bear it until God's timing for it to come to an end.

There hath no temptation taken you but such as is common to man: but God is faithful, who will not suffer you to be tempted above that ye are able; but will with the temptation also make a way to escape, that ye may be able to bear it. (1Corinth.10:13KJV).

The Israelite's two kingdoms Judah (Southern Kingdom) and Ephraim (Northern Kingdom) were allowed by God to be taken into Babylonian and Assyrian captivity because of God's judgement due to their idolatry. His plan was that in their captivity they would come to the realisation of their iniquities and sins against God, repent and be restored to intimacy with Him. He had a plan to cause them to return to their land, Israel during specific times. In the case of Judah, we can read about the period of return in scripture and how following their return, there was a restoration of true worship (Biblical books of Nehemiah and Ezra).

I am also reminded of Job who God allowed Satan to afflict in different devastating ways. Satan was again a "club" or a "tool" in God's hand to test Job's level of faithfulness to God; would he "curse God and die" as his wife advised him to do? God allowed Satan to carry on afflicting Job because He foreknew Job would be able to prevail in great adversity. God knows the measure of affliction we can individually take if God chooses to either test us or chasten us through affliction, so indeed we must as Job, trust him even if we don't understand everything we are going through or the reasons why.

This is what God said about the fate of the King of Assyria after God had used him to afflict God's people and why:
12After the LORD has used the king of Assyria to
accomplish his purposes on Mount Zion and in
Jerusalem, he will turn against the king of Assyria
and punish him—for he is proud and
arrogant. 13He boasts,
"By my own powerful arm I have done this.
With my own shrewd wisdom I planned it.

I have broken down the defenses of nations
and carried off their treasures.
I have knocked down their kings like a bull.
14I have robbed their nests of riches
and gathered up kingdoms as a farmer gathers eggs.
No one can even flap a wing against me
or utter a peep of protest."
15But can the ax boast greater power than the person who uses it?
Is the saw greater than the person who saws?
Can a rod strike unless a hand moves it?
Can a wooden cane walk by itself?
16Therefore, the LORD, the LORD of Heaven's Armies,
will send a plague among Assyria's proud troops,
and a flaming fire will consume its glory.
17The LORD, the Light of Israel, will be a fire;
the Holy One will be a flame.
He will devour the thorns and briers with fire,
burning up the enemy in a single night.
18The LORD will consume Assyria's glory
like a fire consumes a forest in a fruitful land;
it will waste away like sick people in a plague.
19Of all that glorious forest, only a few trees will survive—
so few that a child could count them! (Isaiah 10:12-19 NLT)

In the New Testament we read about what happened to Judas after he betrayed Jesus in exchange for thirty pieces of silver from the religious leaders

(Matt. 26:14-26). His fate was expressed in two parts of scripture:
"Now this man purchased a field with the reward of iniquity; and falling headlong, he burst asunder in the midst, and all his bowels gushed out. And it was known unto all the dwellers at Jerusalem; insomuch as that field is called in their proper tongue, Aceldama, that is to say, The field of blood. For it is written in the book of Psalms, Let his habitation be desolate, and let no man dwell therein: and his bishoprick let another take. (Acts 1:18-20 KJV)
"And he cast down the pieces of silver in the temple, and departed, and went and hanged himself" (Matt. 27:5 KJV)

One thing is certain, offence will come to the people of God for the purpose of pruning and chastening so that they would bear much lasting fruit (John 15) and experience character transformation (James 1:2-4). However woe to those who allow themselves to be "clubs" or "tools" in God's hands to afflict His people:

"Then said he unto the disciples, It is impossible but that offences will come: but woe unto him, through whom they come!" (Luke 17:1 KJV).

Part 2 God's Unlikely Helpers in Paths of Adversity.

There are certain people God will keep in your life all of the time, others He will allow to come for a very short while and to leave soon after as they were merely part of a process of fulfillment of a particular God directed plan. Some however will stay in your life for an extended period until such a time as the purpose for which God sent them is over.

God may allow difficult and offensive people in your life because through them, He plans to transform you by exposing sins, iniquities and weaknesses in you by His Spirit of conviction. This is a blessing because then you can acknowledge your sins in humility and He will fulfil his promise of cleansing you from all unrighteousness (1John 1:9) and prune you so that you bear more lasting fruit (John 15).

It may be that one has a "backpack" full of filthy attitudes, un-forgiveness, compromise in one's Christian walk, hatred or lovelessness that weighs one down preventing one from uprightness before God. He more often than not decides to use situations or Mr or Mrs/Miss so and so through a difficult situation to jolt one back to an upright position of righteousness to reinstate one onto the path He has set to ensure fulfillment of destiny.

Therefore Brethren, in your affliction at the hands of certain people, "LORD have mercy!" is the cry that is likely to penetrate from your lips of anguish and pain, but as God will not leave you nor forsake you when you go through affliction, you will soon be shouting "Hallelujah look what the LORD has done!" when you testify that what appeared as evil has been outworked by God for His good.

God will only smile and say "gotcha!!" for His love and faithfulness knows no bounds. He is a God of strategies who can use the most unlikely people, your enemies, or offenders to bless you! Indeed God always has the last word in the lives of His children!

Chapter 9
God's Faithfulness to the Fully Committed is Guaranteed

When your heart is fully committed to God, every step you take will inevitably be guided and guarded by Him.

"The eyes of the LORD search the whole earth in order to strengthen those whose hearts are fully committed to him..." (2 Chronicles 16:9 KJV).

These are two points to remind you of God's faithfulness to the fully committed, not just by their words but their deeds as well:

1. "*Enter in by the narrow gate; for wide is the gate and broad is the way that leads to destruction, and many are those who enter in by it. Narrow is the gate, and restricted is the way that leads to life! Few are those who find it." (Matt. 7:13-14 KJV).*

The LORD will make sure that you are steered back onto his "narrow" pathway if you should stray away from it at any point due to affliction.

The LORD will be your help in times of trouble to make this possible.

The Psalmist (46:1-3) says "*God is our refuge and strength, a very present help in trouble. Therefore, we won't be afraid, though the earth changes, though the mountains are shaken into the heart of the seas; though its waters roar and are troubled, though the mountains tremble with their swelling. Selah".*

As one who is in fellowship with His Holy Spirit, God will also give you the ability to discern what is of Him and what is not so that you know when you are on a path, He has not led you on.
"So I say, let the Holy Spirit guide your lives. Then you won't be doing what your sinful nature craves. The sinful nature wants to do evil, which is just the opposite of what the Spirit wants. And the Spirit gives us desires that are the opposite of what the sinful nature desires. These two forces are constantly fighting each other, so you are not free to carry out your good intentions." (Gal. 5:16-17 NLT).

God's will is that you live and walk guided by the Holy Spirit not by your own carnal longings and desires which is under the control of Satan who entices the flesh to take the "wide gate" or "broad way". This pathway is pleasing to the flesh or carnal nature because it offers what appear to be easy and quick benefits, in the long term however one realises that the so-called benefits are short lived, resulting in affliction or heartache and discouragement.

2. The LORD will ensure that you part with those you are in alliance with who
i. do not have the same call of God as you do.

ii, are likely to be a hindrance to you one way or another. This is because they are agents of conflict or contention directly or through others associated with them.

Abraham (then called Abram) had left Haran (Gen 12) with his nephew Lot, travelled with him to Egypt where Abraham's riches including livestock had increased. Together Abraham and Lot had a large number of livestock and there came a time that living together and grazing their animals side by side proved difficult as the land was crowded and other communities lived there as well. In addition, their herdsmen had begun to quarrel among themselves. Abraham took the wise decision to separate from Lot saying

"..Is not the whole land before thee? separate thyself, I pray thee, from me: if [thou wilt take] the left hand, then I will go to the right; or if [thou depart] to the right hand, then I will go to the left..." (Gen. 13:9 KJV).

When we study scriptures closely, it is evident that Abraham's call by God out of his country, Haran (Gen. 12) did not include his relatives. He was married at the time, so his wife was included. It was therefore not surprising that a time came for him and Lot to part and what better time than when the land they occupied could not hold their combined possessions.

Today let us pray, asking the LORD to reveal to us if we are aligned to the wrong person, people or group and the wise steps we should take to dissociate ourselves from those He exposes. We need to take care that when God tells us to do something or go a particular way, we are not involving anyone He has not told us to partner with.

Brothers and sisters, when we are fully committed to the LORD, we must partner with Him as He guides and guards our lives, and this means we are to walk in obedience and refuse to compromise with evil. If we know what the truth is according to God's Word, we should refuse at all costs to live by half-truths and lies.

" said Jesus to those Jews which believed on him, If ye continue in my word, [then] are ye my disciples indeed; ye shall know the truth, and the truth shall make you free." (John 8:31-32 KJV).

Today, let us resolve to continue living as dedicated soldiers of Christ marching on fully committed to our commander in chief, our Lord and Saviour Jesus Christ, helping others to stay in line or line up with us as is the will of God.

Chapter 10
God's Standards for Interpersonal Relationships, Do We Conform?

Do you live your life in such a way that you attempt to always be conscious that you are manifesting Christlike behaviour? I would not say that I always do, but it is what I would like to do all the time so I am working on it; As a man thinks in his heart so is he (Prov 23:7), I therefore believe that I can do all things through Christ who strengthens me.

Impartiality and love towards one another is high on God's list of things that pleases Him because He is a God of relationship.

"The poor are despised even by their neighbors, while the rich have many friends."
It is a sin to belittle one's neighbor; blessed are those who help the poor." (Prov.14:20-21 NLT).

In Proverbs 14: 20-21, God is speaking to us through His Word about the type of person He blesses; one who does not despise the poor but rather helps them. A "poor neighbour" in this context is a person who may literally live next to someone or know that person who sees themselves as more superior than them because they are richer.

The "superior" one despises them and does not want to associate with them simply because they are poor or less well off. This kind of "I am better than you because of my economic status" behaviour or attitude is not often deliberate or conscious; it is often inbred and rooted in upbringing as well as the innate Adamic nature that tends to conform to ungodly societal norms and reasoning.

It is however not the kind of attitude or reasoning befitting a member of the Kingdom of God or truly born-again believers in Christ. We must not conform to the world's class distinctions or how to behave towards people who are different to us in anyway, be it economically, socially, racially or culturally.

The meaning of "despise" is to look down on or to loathe and the opposite of despise is love, cherish, or appreciate. God requires us to love, cherish and appreciate our fellow human being whether they are Christians or not and regardless of their background.

In fact, James expresses true religion as such *"pure and genuine religion in the sight of God the Father means caring for orphans and widows in their distress and refusing to let the world corrupt you." (James 1:27NLT).*

God does not only assess Christian character according to the degree of holiness in the traditional sense of the word i.e. overcoming sinful acts like hatred, un-forgiveness, and sexual immorality, but also according to the way we treat one another, especially the less fortunate or more vulnerable and needy.

Jesus also said that whatever care is given to the needy (e.g. feeding the hungry, giving drink to the thirsty and caring for the sick) is as if it is done unto him. Those who do this are counted among his true disciples or "Sheep" (Mathew 25:31-46).

Indeed, the way we relate to one another that pleases God is defined as true godliness and reaps heavenly rewards and affirms our salvation.

When we demonstrate our love to the "poor neighbour" by affirming them as being significant and helping them, God blesses us (Prov.14:21). This is in fact obeying the two greatest commandments which is to love God and others (Deut. 6:4-5/Matthew 22:36-40). It is our Love for God that compels us to love ourselves the way He loves us (we need to receive His love) and as a result we can express love or compassion towards others. This is what I call the cyclical or "domino effect" love bond of the New Covenant. When we are in Christ, we are expected to love as God loves for He is Love (1John 4:8).

May God help us to be perfected in His sacrificial and unconditional love so that we demonstrate it to our brethren and the unsaved!

The apostle Paul said "*There is no longer Jew or Gentile, slave or free, male and female. For you are all one in Christ Jesus." (Gal.3:28 NLT).*

This verse refers to the Kingdom of God as having people of all races, backgrounds, nationalities, cultures, social/economic status and genders. What we must also realise is that it indirectly refers to the kind of mindset expected of this melange of God's people.

Those who belong to Christ are ones with a Kingdom mind-set that says "all these people within the Body of Christ are united with me and I with them through Christ and therefore in God's eyes we are all of equal worth" and such a mind-set is in agreement with the following statement "If I came into the Christian faith with prejudices in relation to certain races, cultures, nationalities or "classes" of people, I must acknowledge and confess these sins and ask God for forgiveness."

"But if we confess our sins to him, he is faithful and just to forgive us our sins and to cleanse us from all wickedness." (1 John 1:9 NLT)

It is worth noting that many people are wounded because of afflictions in interpersonal relationships or past family problems so that although in Christ, and desire to, (because we are one in God's love) they fail to express the God kind of love to others.

We cannot love, forgive or overcome prejudices and learnt behaviour that causes us to mistreat others in our own strength. We must speak to God honestly about our weaknesses and trust him. This is a sign of obedience and humility which pleases Him and results in His manifested presence (John 14:21, 23/1 Peter 5:5).

God is able and willing to transform our lives by delivering us from mind sets and attitudes of the world and healing us physically, emotionally, mentally, and psychologically. Isaiah 61:1-3 reminds us of God's transforming power through Christ:

For more information:
Bearwitness-Forerunner Ministries International

Email: bearwitnessforerunner88@gmail.com

ISBN: 978-1-9163509-7-7

www.ingramcontent.com/pod-product-compliance
Lightning Source LLC
LaVergne TN
LVHW010117170826
845678LV00012B/2461